Snails

By Heather Hammonds

Illustrations by Jenny Mountstephen

Contents

Snail Trails

"Oh, no!" I said to Tia, one morning.
"Look at our lettuces."

We were growing lettuces in a tub at home,
in the spring.
There were green ones and red ones
and ones with crinkly leaves.

Now some of our lettuces had big holes in their leaves.

"I wonder how those holes got there," said Tia.

The next day, there were more holes in our lettuces.

“I think something has been eating them,” I said.

“Let’s ask Dad what to do,” said Tia.

Dad looked at our lettuces.

"Aha!" he said. "Can you see the silver marks on the lettuce leaves?"

"Yes," I said.

"Those are snail trails," said Dad.

We began to follow the snail trails.
They went down the side of the tub,
across the path and under some rocks.

Dad carefully lifted up one of the rocks.

"Look at those snails!" I gasped.

There were lots of little snails under the rocks.

"Let's put them in a bucket
and take them to the park," said Tia.
"They can eat grass and leaves there."

"Then our lettuces won't get any more holes in their leaves!" I said, happily.

All About Snails

Snails are small animals with soft bodies.
They have no backbone.
They have hard shells to protect their bodies.

There are many different types of snails.
Some snails live on land
and some snails live in water.

All snails have four tentacles on their heads.
They have eyes on the longest tentacles.

Snails also have lots of little spiky teeth
on a pad in their mouth.
The pad is called a radula.

A snail eats with its radula.

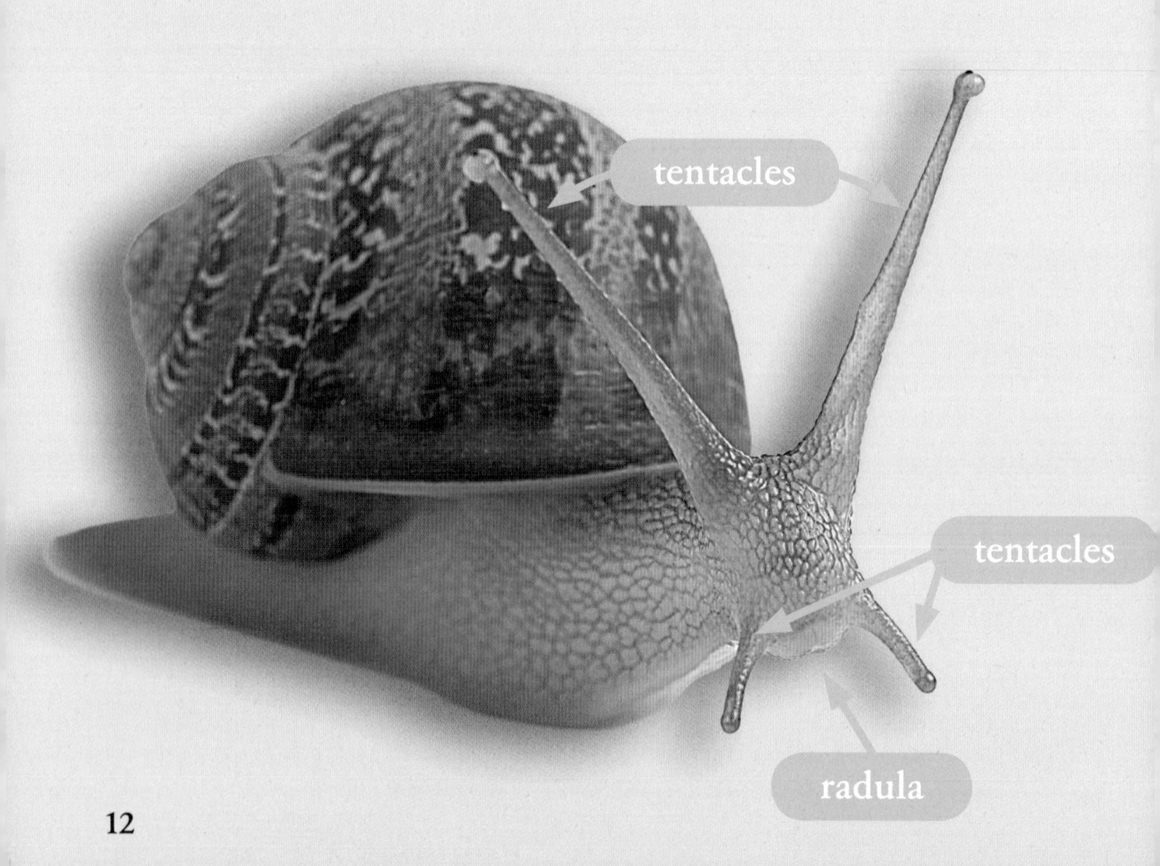

Snails move using a big 'foot'.
Land snails make silvery slime,
called mucus, in their foot.
The mucus helps them to move
along the ground.

Land snails live under rocks
and in other damp, dark places.
Sometimes, many snails live in the one place.

Snails move around at night,
or when it is wet.

On sunny days, snails stay out of the sun.

Land snails eat leaves, moss and other plant materials.

Sometimes, snails are pests because they eat plants in people's gardens.